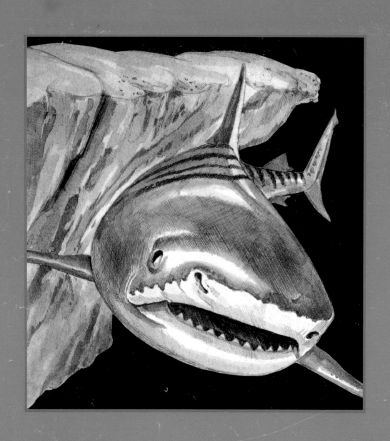

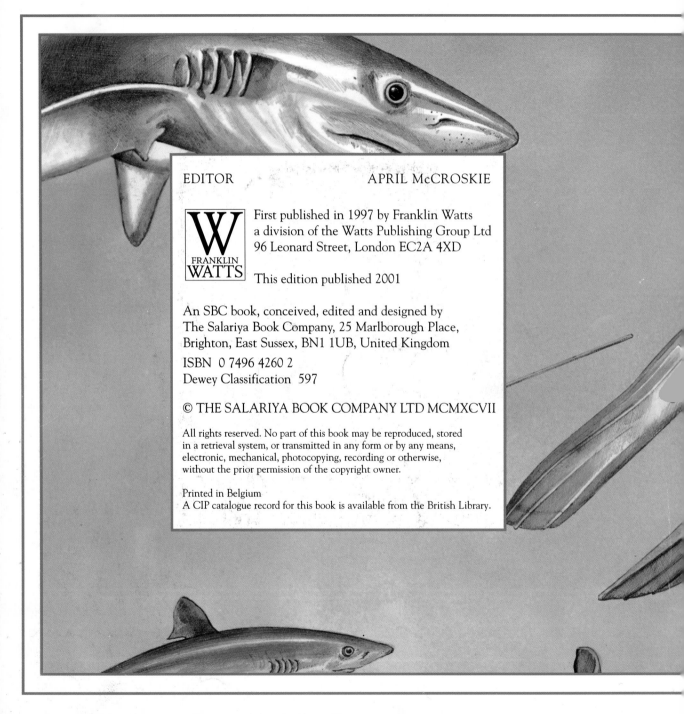

EDITOR   APRIL McCROSKIE

W FRANKLIN **WATTS**

First published in 1997 by Franklin Watts
a division of the Watts Publishing Group Ltd
96 Leonard Street, London EC2A 4XD

This edition published 2001

An SBC book, conceived, edited and designed by
The Salariya Book Company, 25 Marlborough Place,
Brighton, East Sussex, BN1 1UB, United Kingdom
ISBN 0 7496 4260 2
Dewey Classification 597

Printed in Belgium
A CIP catalogue record for this book is available from the British Library.

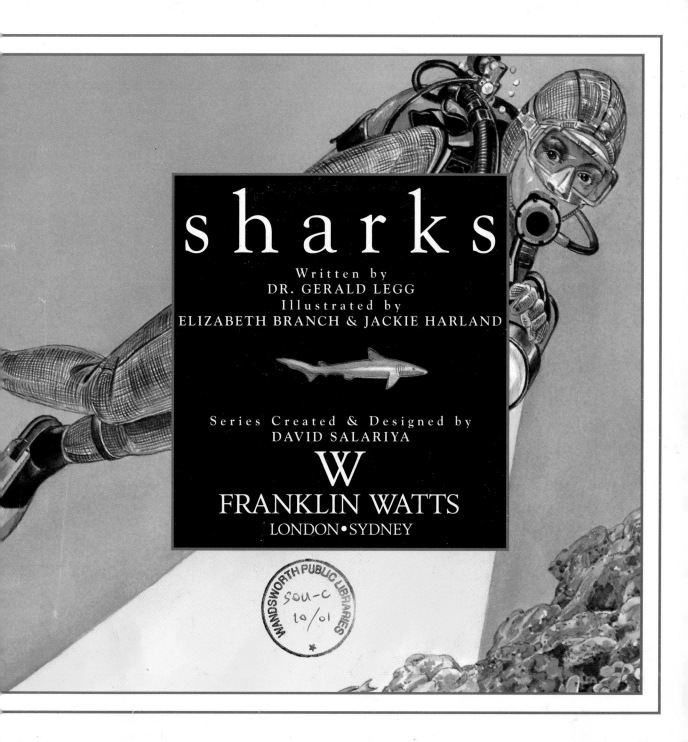

sharks

Written by
DR. GERALD LEGG
Illustrated by
ELIZABETH BRANCH & JACKIE HARLAND

Series Created & Designed by
DAVID SALARIYA

W
FRANKLIN WATTS
LONDON • SYDNEY

CONTENTS

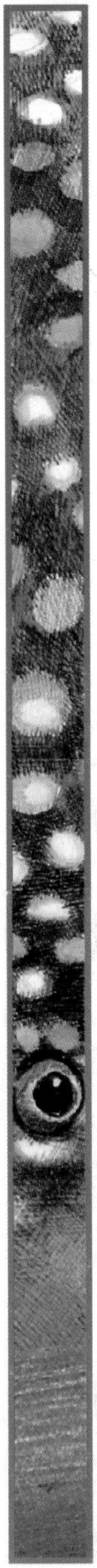

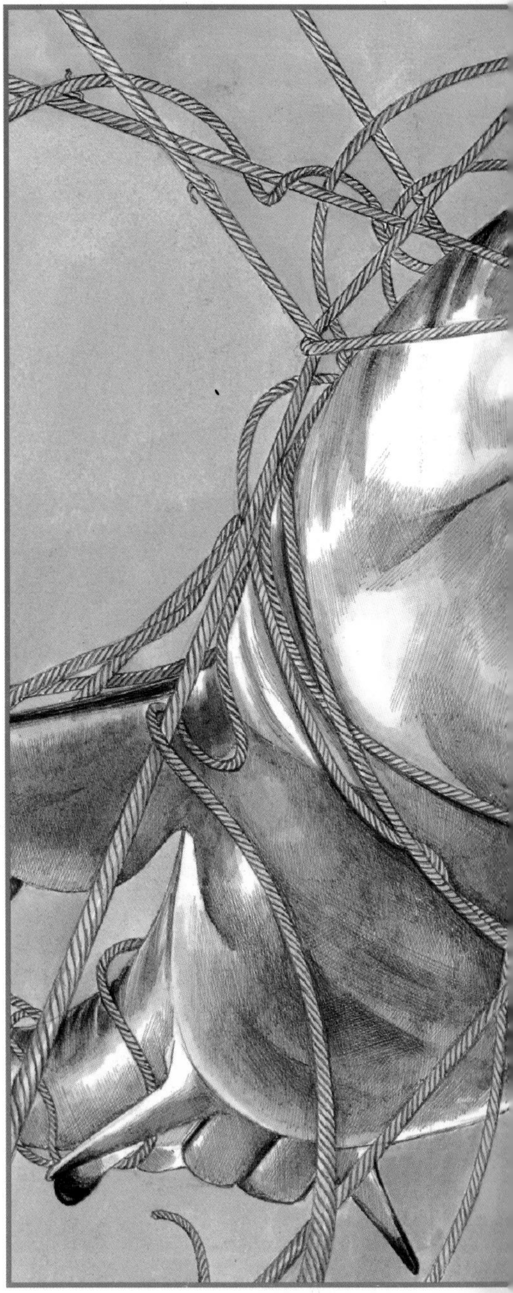

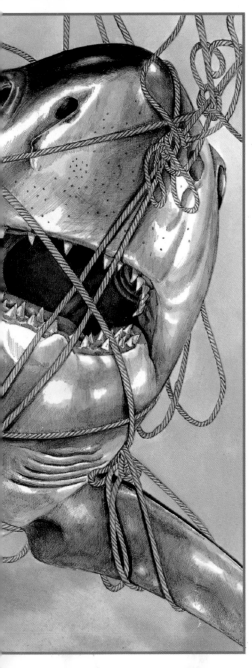

Shark!

The perfect killing machine and most feared inhabitant of the seas. Over 450 million years of evolution have produced a very efficient creature. There are huge sharks over 4.5 metres long and tiny 15-centimetre long species. Most have sharp teeth to cut up their food, but some have flat ones for grinding up molluscs. Strangely, the largest sharks have hardly any teeth. They feed upon microscopic animal life. There are over 300 species living in the oceans, near coral reefs and even venturing into rivers. But they are still mysterious creatures.

Tail fin

Dorsal fin

Second dorsal fin

Skates and rays are relatives of sharks and also have skeletons made of cartilage.

Anal fin

Sharks

are unique. Unlike fish who have skeletons of bone, their skeleton is made of rubbery cartilage. They do not have the special air-sac that other fish have to stop them sinking, and many sharks produce live young rather than eggs.

The spiral valve of some sharks (left) makes spiral faeces.

Pectoral fin

Spotted eagle ray

Skate

Torpedo ray

Chimaera, another shark relative

Most sharks have sharp teeth, but some have flattened teeth to crush their prey. All skates and rays are crushers with flattened teeth.

A large brain (right) means that sharks are clever and alert.

Mouth

Eye

Shark skin is covered in tiny overlapping scales.

Sharks have a broad mouth with rows of teeth which are replaced as they wear out.

Saw shark

Smooth hound shark

Blind shark

Angel shark

Barbeled-hound shark

Wobbegong shark

False cat shark

Bramble shark

Bamboo shark

Dogfish shark

Finback cat shark

Whale shark

Cat shark

Rough shark

Nurse shark

Frilled shark

Hammerhead shark

Zebra shark

Cow shark

Requiem shark

Thresher shark

Horn shark

Weasel shark

Mackerel shark

Collared carpet shark

Sand tiger shark

Basking shark

Megamouth shark

Crocodile shark

Goblin shark

Sharks are elegant, streamlined, fast and alert. Most are underwater hunters and are found throughout the world. But some just live on the seabed and eat shellfish.

Sharks can be identified by the shapes of their teeth.

With jaws open a great white lunges forward to bite lumps of flesh from large fish (below). Other food on the menu includes seals, penguins, swimmers and even other sharks.

Bull shark

Sand shark

Lemon shark

Tiger shark

Mako shark

Dusky shark

Some sharks, like the white pointer, have saw-like teeth ideal for biting out chunks of thick flesh.

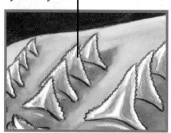

Another name for the feared great white shark is white death.

The mako shark has massive cutting teeth. It is a fierce hunter able to catch fast-swimming swordfish weighing 50 kilograms. They will attack people and even fishing boats.

Mako shark

Sharks are swift and agile, and are armed with rows of razor-sharp cutting teeth. To find and follow its prey a shark sways its head from side to side. Many sharks approach, unseen, from behind or below. They swoop in and take a bite, then move away briefly before returning to feed. Once bitten the victim becomes weak through shock and blood loss. Many sharks will nudge their prey, testing it, before biting. But the great white attacks hard and fast, tearing its prey to pieces.

The long, curved teeth of a sand tiger shark get smaller from the middle to the sides of the jaw making them ideal for catching slippery fish and squid.

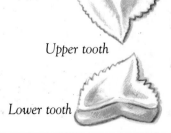

Upper tooth

Lower tooth

11

Mussels are shellfish that live within two strong, hard shells. But they are not strong enough to keep out a horn shark.

A few sharks prefer to eat shellfish. Monkfish and horn sharks, like the bullhead shark and the Port Jackson shark, have special teeth and jaws for breaking open shellfish such as sea urchins, mussels and crabs. These sharks' bodies are flattened and well-camouflaged for living on the seabed.

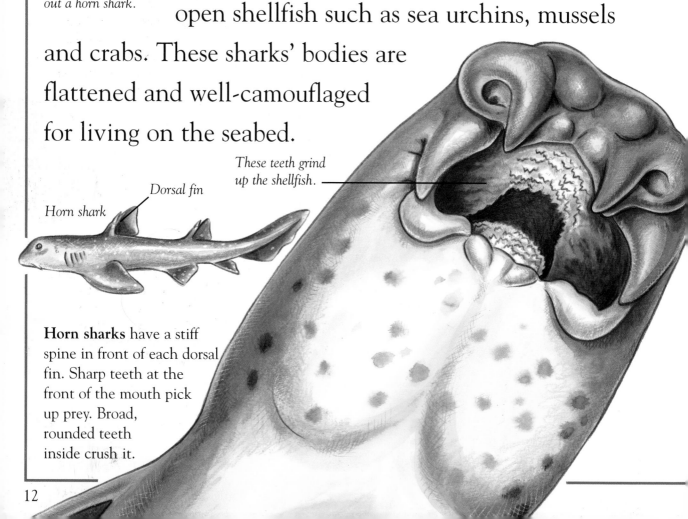

These teeth grind up the shellfish.

Dorsal fin

Horn shark

Horn sharks have a stiff spine in front of each dorsal fin. Sharp teeth at the front of the mouth pick up prey. Broad, rounded teeth inside crush it.

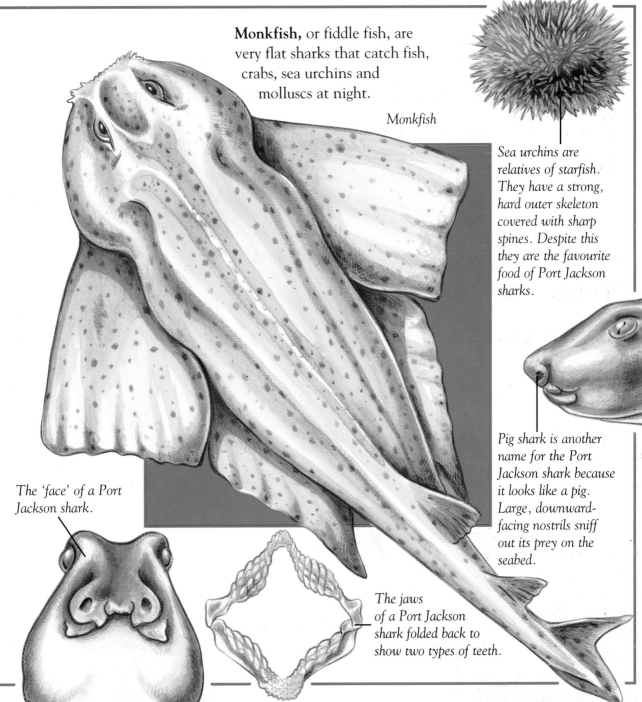

Monkfish, or fiddle fish, are very flat sharks that catch fish, crabs, sea urchins and molluscs at night.

Monkfish

Sea urchins are relatives of starfish. They have a strong, hard outer skeleton covered with sharp spines. Despite this they are the favourite food of Port Jackson sharks.

Pig shark is another name for the Port Jackson shark because it looks like a pig. Large, downward-facing nostrils sniff out its prey on the seabed.

The 'face' of a Port Jackson shark.

The jaws of a Port Jackson shark folded back to show two types of teeth.

Near the surface millions of tiny plants and animals live in every cubic metre of water. They are called plankton.

The largest sharks alive today are basking sharks and whale sharks. They gulp huge amounts of water, catching small fish and microscopic plankton to eat. To help them float they have a huge oil-filled liver.

Fishing in groups of two or more, basking sharks take in nearly 9,000 litres (over 9 tonnes) of water an hour. Five huge gills filter out the plankton which these giant sharks eat.

The largest living fish is the whale shark, weighing around 20 tonnes and measuring over 15 metres. They live on their own.

Whale shark

When they are frightened the powerful muscular body, large tail, and stiff fins allow the shark to swim at speed.

Whale sharks live in tropical seas where they usually feed vertically in the water. They rise up out of the water then sink slowly with their wide mouth open, sucking in shoals of small fish. Basking sharks sometimes feed like this too. Little else is known about them except that they lay eggs 30 centimetres long.

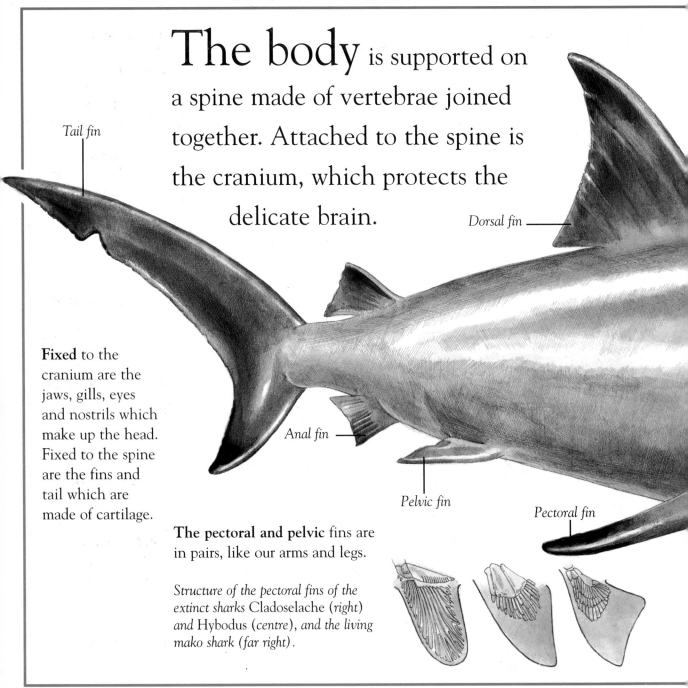

The body is supported on a spine made of vertebrae joined together. Attached to the spine is the cranium, which protects the delicate brain.

Tail fin

Dorsal fin

Fixed to the cranium are the jaws, gills, eyes and nostrils which make up the head. Fixed to the spine are the fins and tail which are made of cartilage.

Anal fin

Pelvic fin

Pectoral fin

The pectoral and pelvic fins are in pairs, like our arms and legs.

Structure of the pectoral fins of the extinct sharks Cladoselache (right) *and* Hybodus (centre), *and the living mako shark (far right).*

THE STRUCTURE OF A SHARK

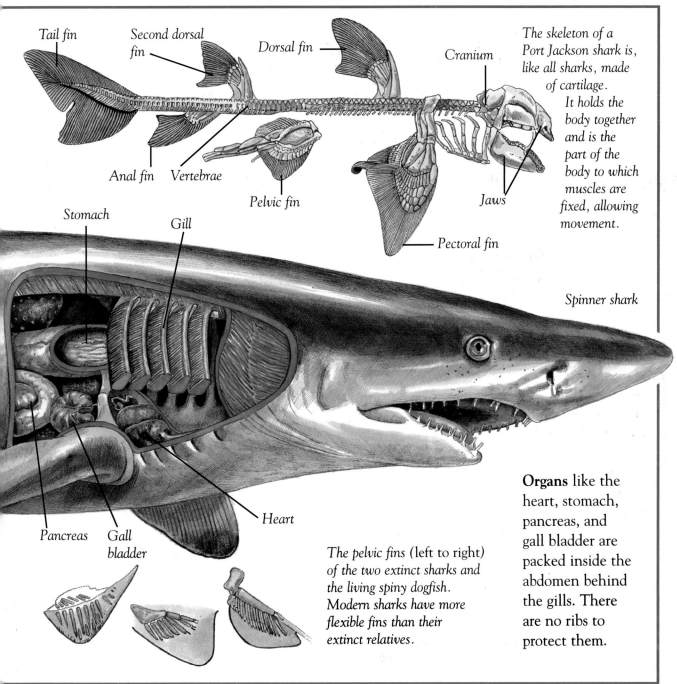

Tail fin

Second dorsal fin

Dorsal fin

Cranium

The skeleton of a Port Jackson shark is, like all sharks, made of cartilage.

It holds the body together and is the part of the body to which muscles are fixed, allowing movement.

Anal fin

Vertebrae

Pelvic fin

Jaws

Pectoral fin

Stomach

Gill

Spinner shark

Pancreas

Gall bladder

Heart

The pelvic fins (left to right) of the two extinct sharks and the living spiny dogfish. Modern sharks have more flexible fins than their extinct relatives.

Organs like the heart, stomach, pancreas, and gall bladder are packed inside the abdomen behind the gills. There are no ribs to protect them.

How do sharks swim? Muscles contract (tighten) on one side of the body, followed half a second later by muscles on the other side. This action bends the body so water is forced backwards and the shark travels forwards.

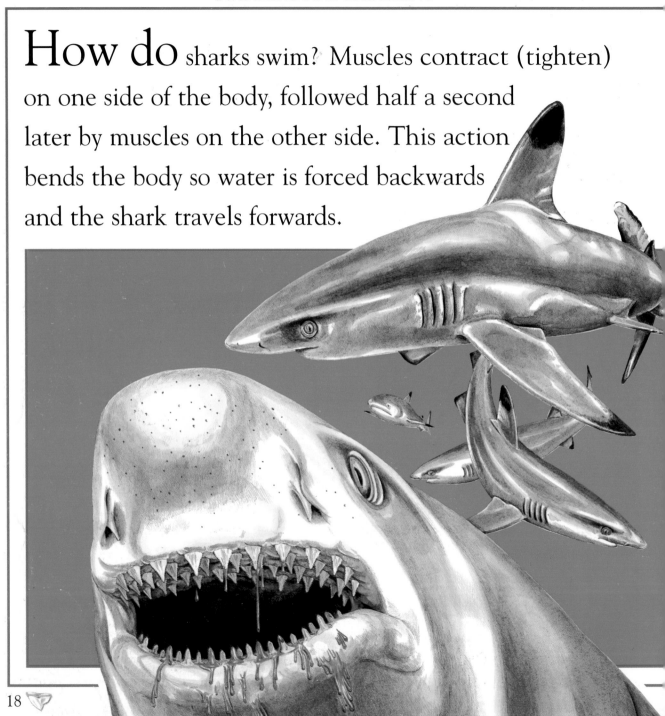

If a shark stops swimming it sinks and drowns.
Its oily liver also helps it float. The pectoral fins,
which stick out from the shark's sides,
force it up as it moves. Breathing occurs
as water flows through the gills.

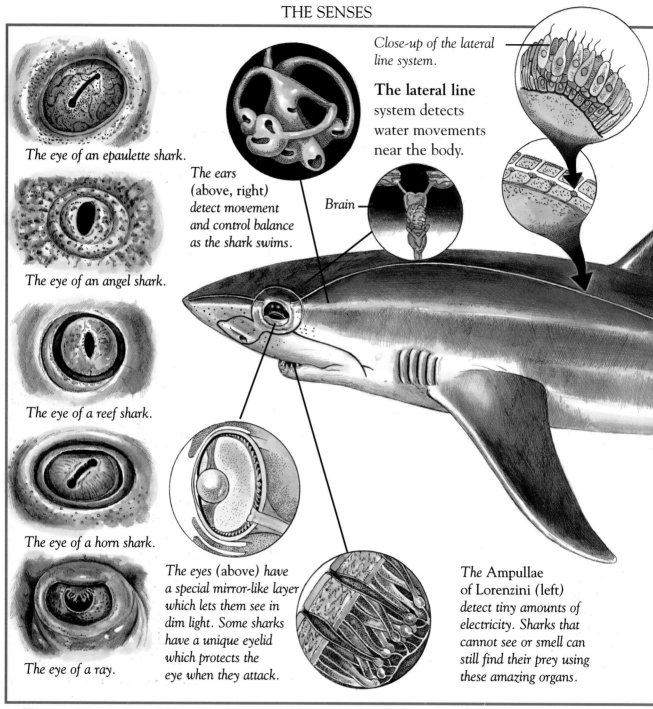

The eye of an epaulette shark.

The eye of an angel shark.

The eye of a reef shark.

The eye of a horn shark.

The eye of a ray.

Close-up of the lateral line system.

The lateral line system detects water movements near the body.

The ears (above, right) detect movement and control balance as the shark swims.

Brain

The eyes (above) have a special mirror-like layer which lets them see in dim light. Some sharks have a unique eyelid which protects the eye when they attack.

The Ampullae of Lorenzini (left) detect tiny amounts of electricity. Sharks that cannot see or smell can still find their prey using these amazing organs.

Sharks have an amazingly complicated sensory system that lets them see, hear, smell, taste and feel. Unlike humans they can also detect tiny amounts of electricity, and probably other things that we do not yet know about. Even in murky water a shark knows exactly what is going on around it.

These are pit organs (right). We do not know what they do but perhaps they sense movement, sound or taste.

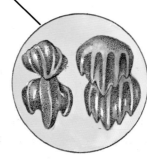

Sharks are able to detect electricity and low notes of sound in the sea. This helps them to find their prey since the muscles of a swimming animal make a noise which sharks can hear. Electricity and sound also help sharks navigate.

Covered in spots, a camouflaged Leopold shark (right) rests on the seabed waiting to rush at its prey.

A pale-coloured belly changing to dark blue. This is called counter shading and disguises the slender blue shark.

The sides and back of a tiger shark are covered in a pattern of broken bars. This makes it almost invisible among the reefs.

Shark and prey play hide-and-seek. Each tries to remain invisible from the other. Their colour and body shape match the environment making them 'disappear'.

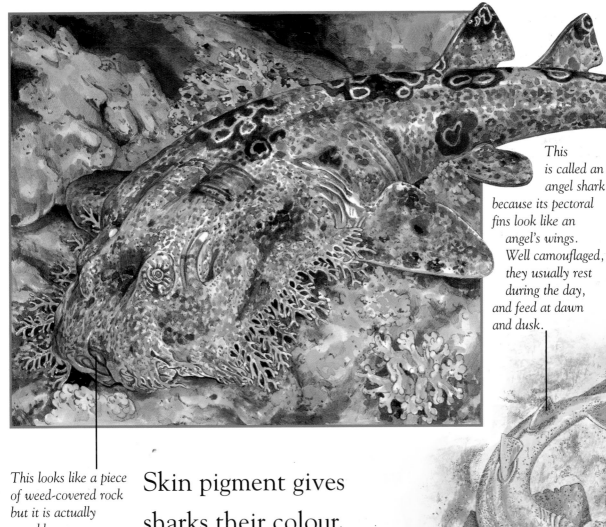

This is called an angel shark because its pectoral fins look like an angel's wings. Well camouflaged, they usually rest during the day, and feed at dawn and dusk.

This looks like a piece of weed-covered rock but it is actually a wobbegong or carpet shark. These lie partly buried in the sand waiting to suck in passing fish or crabs.

Skin pigment gives sharks their colour. Many are blue-grey, like the colour of the surrounding water.

Sharks scare people. Because of this they are even worshipped in some parts of the world. It is likely that 1,000 people are attacked by sharks every year. The great white has the worst reputation which is why it is called 'white death'. Most sharks are harmless but even so it is safer not to swim where sharks are swimming. For protection, beaches can be fenced off, or electric barriers can be used. But swimmers can usually fend off a shark with a punch to its nose.

Grey reef sharks in a feeding frenzy. Sharks gather where a kill has been made.

The blood over excites the sharks to the extent that they may attack each other.

When frightened, the swell shark inflates its body and wedges itself into rocky crevices. Spiny scales hold it firmly in place.

Bites from the cookie cutter shark can make holes in the rubber coating of submarines.

Cookie cutter

We know very little about sharks' habits. With over 300 species there is a lot to learn. They attack people, but why do they only do this sometimes?

If you turn a shark upside down it goes limp. This means it is asleep.

Remora are fish with a sucker on their head to hold onto sharks. They help the shark by eating parasites on its skin.

Some sharks swim across seas, and others stay in the same area. Some gather together to sleep in caves but why don't they drown if they are not moving? Some have lights on their body – do these help them find food?

Male sharks

may swim a long way to find females. Fertilisation is internal, unlike most fish which shed eggs and sperm into the surrounding water. After fertilisation the eggs are laid, hidden amongst weeds and rocks. Some sharks keep their eggs inside their body where they hatch into baby sharks called pups.

The egg cases of the Port Jackson shark are screw-shaped. The female screws them firmly into rock crevices to hide them from predators.

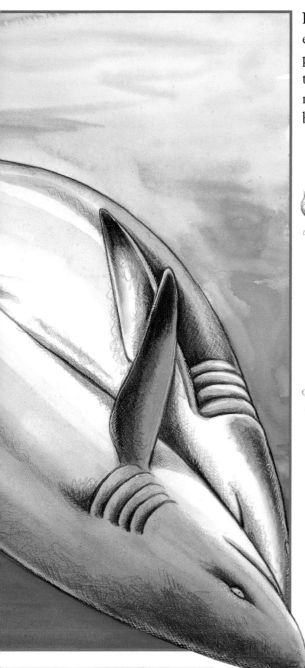

Female sharks have extra thick skin to protect themselves from the males. Once coupled, mating sharks lie side by side.

Shark eggs are protected inside a leathery case. The tiny embryo grows, feeding on the yolk that fills the case.

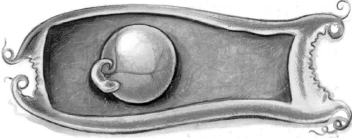

Embryo at one month

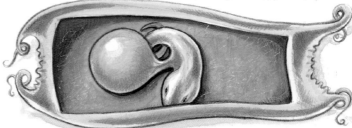

Embryo at three months

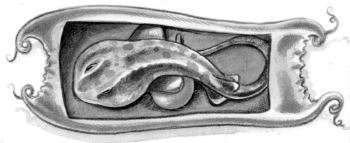

Embryo at seven months

Some sharks roam the ocean, far away from land.

Many sharks live hidden in the ocean depths.

Lantern shark

The lantern shark lives deep in the ocean, at a depth of around 2,000 metres. It has small light-organs on its belly.

Many sharks are to be found in the warm seas of the tropics and subtropics – especially close to land and near the water's surface.

The bull shark is a tropical species found worldwide. It lives near shores and may enter rivers. It also attacks humans.

Ocean-going sharks include the agile mako (*above*) which is found all over the world. Its dorsal fin can be seen sticking up above the water as it swims. It has been known to bite boats, leaving behind its teeth.

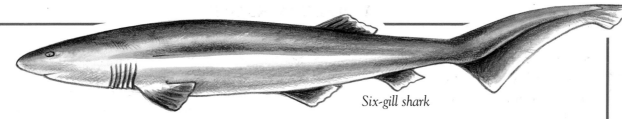
Six-gill shark

Sharks can be found in every ocean and sea. Some live in shallow water, others in the ocean depths. They may live on their own or in groups. Groups of sharks consist of either males or females. The two sexes only meet in the breeding season. Each group has sharks of around the same size, because smaller sharks would soon be eaten by the bigger ones.

Thresher shark

The six-gill shark dives down to 1,850 metres where it rests on the seabed. It surfaces at night to feed.

The thresher shark is found all over the world. It grows to 6 metres, half of which is tail length.

The smallest shark is the dwarf shark at only 15 centimetres long. It is found in the Pacific.

Dwarf shark

For hundreds of years sharks' teeth have been made into jewellery. Nowadays they are sold to tourists.

Thousands of sharks are killed by becoming tangled in fishing nets (*right*) and the nets which protect swimmers from sharks.

Sharks are hunted for many reasons. Some people think it is brave and clever to hunt them for 'sport'. They are also caught commercially for their meat, which is eaten or used as fertiliser. Oil from their liver is used in cosmetics, medicines and in industry. Shark skin makes fine leather. Many sharks are becoming rare and they need protection.

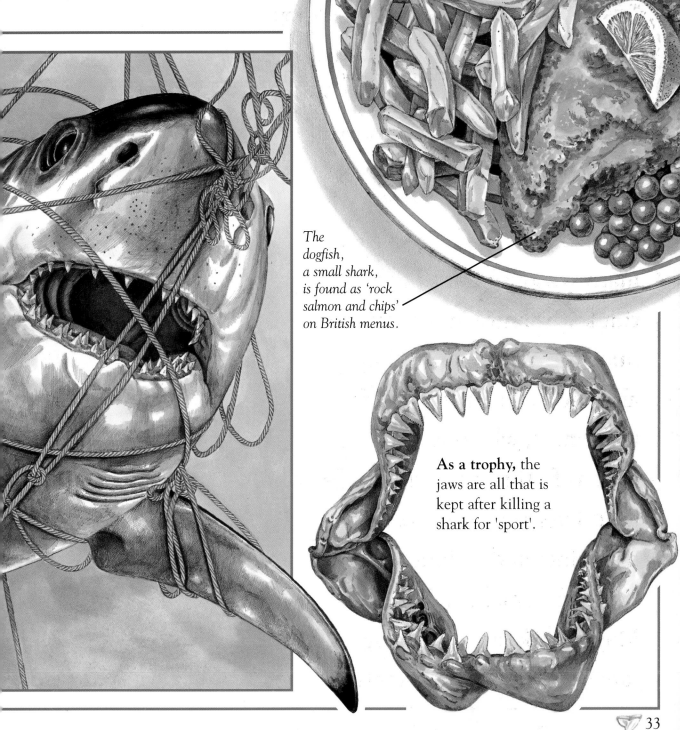

The
dogfish,
a small shark,
is found as 'rock
salmon and chips'
on British menus.

As a trophy, the jaws are all that is kept after killing a shark for 'sport'.

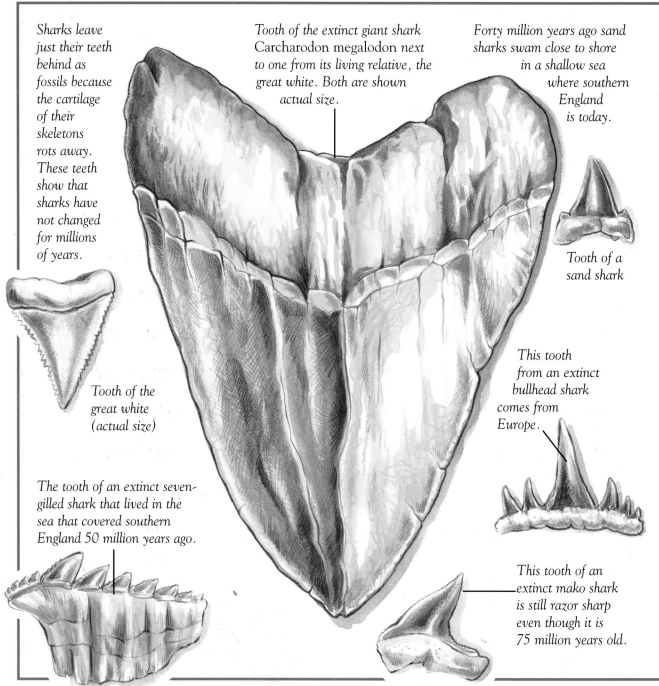

Sharks leave just their teeth behind as fossils because the cartilage of their skeletons rots away. These teeth show that sharks have not changed for millions of years.

Tooth of the extinct giant shark Carcharodon megalodon *next to one from its living relative, the great white. Both are shown actual size.*

Forty million years ago sand sharks swam close to shore in a shallow sea where southern England is today.

Tooth of a sand shark

Tooth of the great white (actual size)

This tooth from an extinct bullhead shark comes from Europe.

The tooth of an extinct seven-gilled shark that lived in the sea that covered southern England 50 million years ago.

This tooth of an extinct mako shark is still razor sharp even though it is 75 million years old.

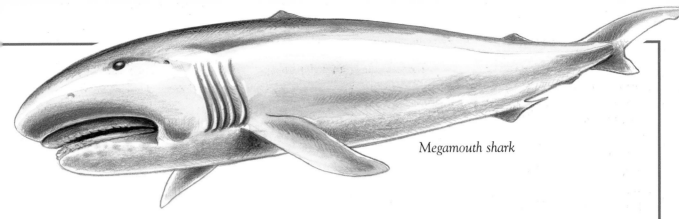

Megamouth shark

The 4.5-metre- long megamouth shark is the most recently found shark. It was discovered in 1976, caught in the anchor of an American ship.

The remains of the oldest shark date back 450 million years. Streamlined and sleek, the 2-metre-long *Cladoselache* was a common shark.

Fossils show us that some sharks have not changed for hundreds of millions of years. The frilled shark, for example, lived around 350 million years ago. Some sharks were huge. *Carcharodon megalodon* must have weighed 20 tonnes and been over 17 metres long. It only became extinct 11,000 years ago. As well as fossil sharks, new species continue to be discovered.

The extinct Cladoselache

For sharks to survive it is important for us to know as much as possible about them. They are difficult to keep alive in captivity so they have to be studied in the wild. But special equipment is needed. Sharks are scared easily and swim away quickly from scientists. But by using bait, sharks can be caught and tagged with numbers, flags and transmitters that allow them to be tracked. Books, films, television and marine centres help us learn more.

Tagged sharks can be followed as they go about their daily lives.

A diver studies a shark from the safety of a metal cage (above).

Scientists use a special craft to explore the oceans' depths. Inside this they can study the deep-water sharks.

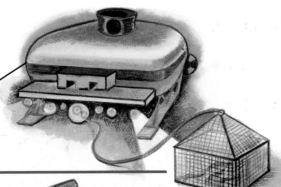

A diver inside a plastic box can follow and study sharks in safety.

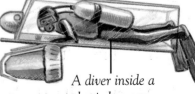

USEFUL WORDS

Camouflage
When an animal uses its colour and shape to pretend to be part of its surroundings.

Embryo Growing baby before it hatches or is born.

Evolution The development of a plant or animal over millions of years.

Extinct Dead and gone forever.

Fertilisation The joining of male sperm and female eggs to produce young.

Fossil Remains of an ancient animal or plant buried in rock and often turned to stone.

Gills The organs used by sharks and fish to breathe.

Mating When a male and a female join together to have young.

Microscopic Tiny and invisible to the naked eye.

Mollusc An animal that has a soft body and usually a hard outer shell, such as mussels and oysters.

Parasite An animal or plant that lives off another animal or plant.

Pigment
Colouring in the skin of an animal.

Predator An animal that hunts other animals for food.

Prey Animals that are hunted as food by other animals.

Species A group of living things that share similar characteristics.

Subtropics and Tropics Coming from a very hot place in the world near the Equator.

Vertebrae The segments which make up the backbone.

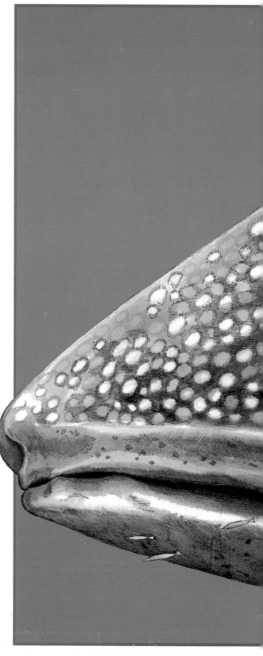

INDEX

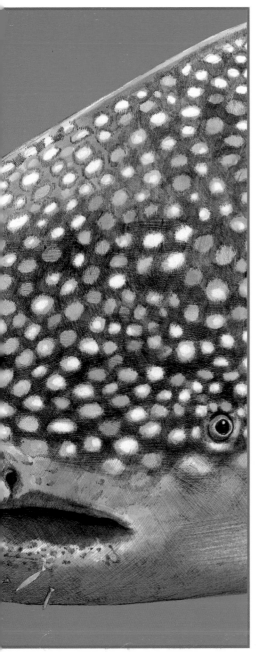